Grades 1–5   Double bass

Improve your sight-reading!

Paul Harris

Grade 1

Stage 1   **G major or F major**   ♩ ♩ 4/4   *page 2*

Stage 2   **D major or B♭ major**   𝄽 3/4   *page 6*

Stage 3   **Dynamic markings**   ♫ 2/4   *page 10*

Grade 2

Stage 1   **G and D major, 2-note slurs**   *page 13*

Stage 2   **A natural minor, C major**   ♩. ─   *page 16*

Stage 3   **Revision**   ─────   *page 19*

Grade 3

Stage 1   **F major (half position), ties**   ♩. ♪   *page 22*

Stage 2   **B♭ major**   ♫♫   *page 25*

Stage 3   **B minor, staccato and pizzicato**   ♩. ♩   *page 28*

Grade 4

Stage 1   **A major, shifting to 3rd position, upbeats**   ♪   *page 31*

Stage 2   **6/8 rhythm patterns, D minor**   *page 34*

Stage 3   **More 6/8 rhythm patterns, E minor**   *page 37*

Grade 5

Stage 1   **Dotted rhythms in 6/8, more shifting**   *page 40*

Stage 2   **G minor**   *page 43*

Stage 3   **Simple syncopation**   *page 46*

ff FABER MUSIC

Grade 1 Stage 1

G or F major

Rhythmic exercises

Always practise the rhythmic exercises carefully before going on. There are different ways of doing these exercises:
- Your teacher (or a metronome) taps the lower line while you clap or tap the upper line.
- You tap the lower line with your foot and clap or tap the upper line with your hands.
- You tap one line with one hand and the other line with the other hand on a table top.
- You tap the lower line and sing the upper line.

Before you begin each exercise count two bars in – one out loud and one silently.

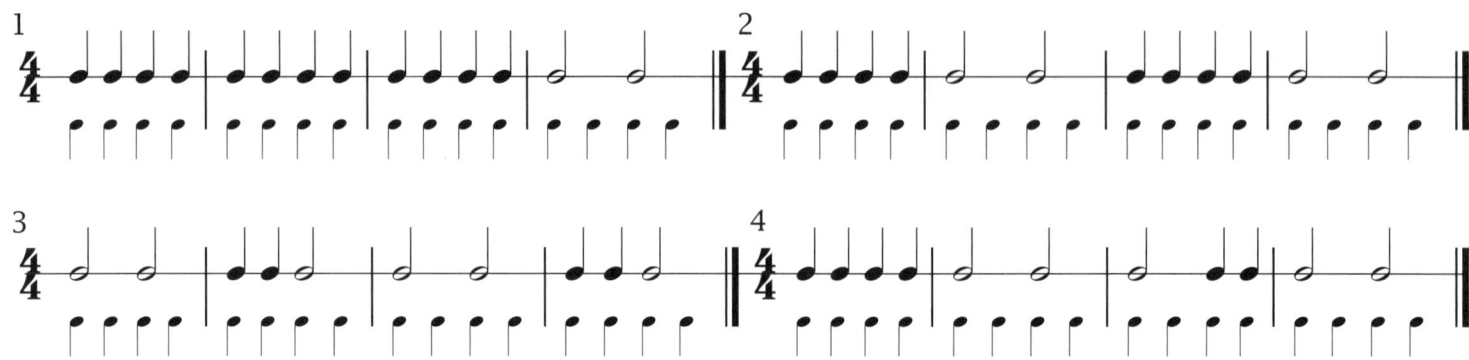

Melodic exercises

Set 1: First position (G major)

Hear each exercise in your head before you play it.

1 
2 
3 
4 
5 
6

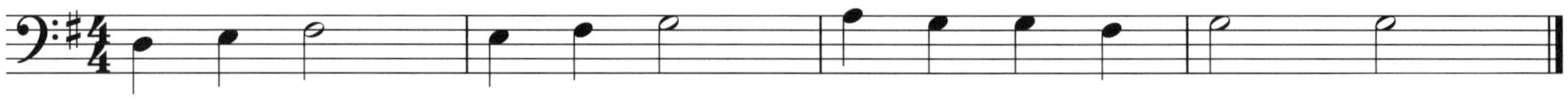

Grade 1 Stage 1

Set 2: Half position (F major)

Prepared piece (first position)

1. How many beats are there in each bar? What will you count?
2. What is the key? Play the scale.
3. What do bars 1 and 3, and 2 and 4 have in common?
4. Play a G (the first note) then hear the piece in your head.
5. How will you put some character into your performance?

1

Prepared piece (half position)

1. How will you count this piece?
2. Tap the rhythm then (tapping the pulse) hear the rhythm in your head.
3. What is the key? Play the scale.
4. Compare bar 1 with bar 3.
5. How will you put some character into your performance?

2

Improvise!

1

Make up your own piece (it can be as long or short as you like), beginning with one of these patterns. Make sure you keep the pulse steady

2

Now make up your own piece in G major or F major, using any patterns you like.

Grade 1 Stage 1

Going solo!

Remember to prepare each piece carefully before you play it.

Grade 1 Stage 2

D or B♭ major

Rhythmic exercises

Always remember to count two bars in.

1

2

3

4

5

6 Write your own rhythmic exercise, then clap it.

Melodic exercises

Set 1: First position (D major)

1

2

3

4

5

6

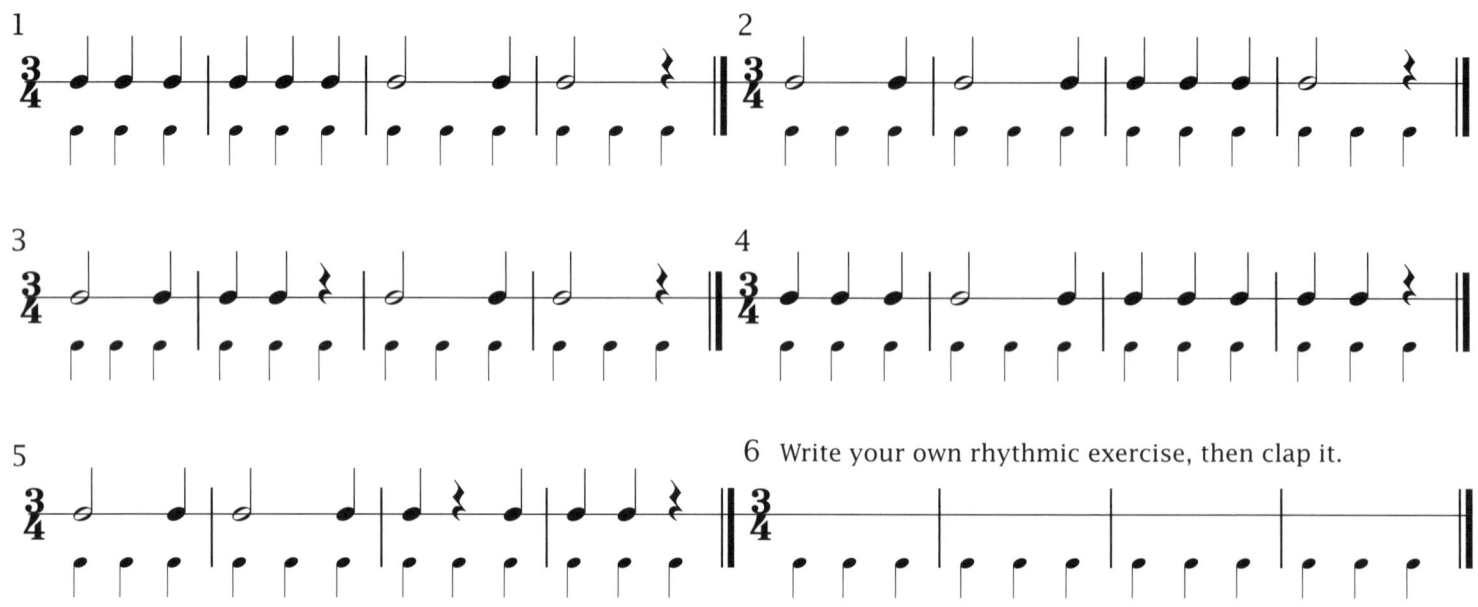

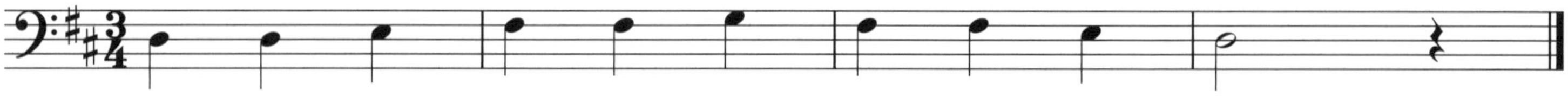

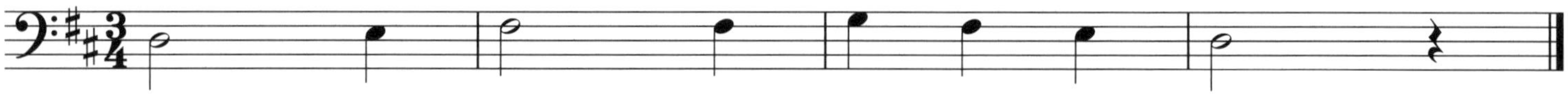

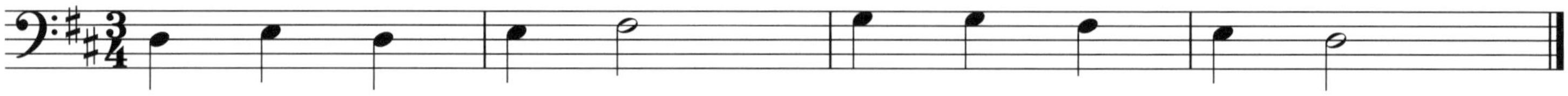

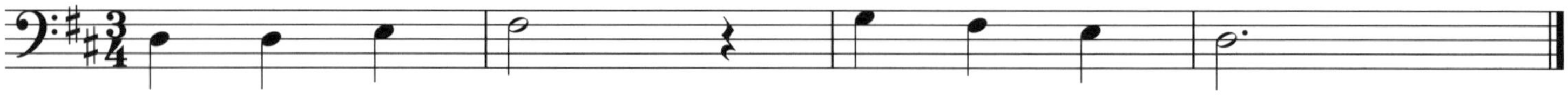

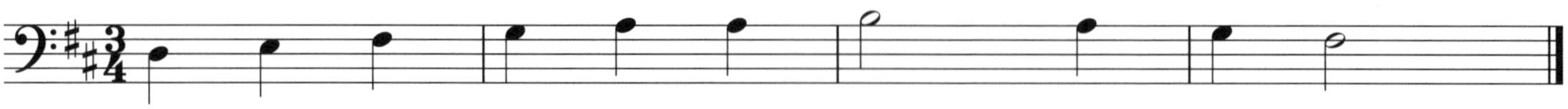

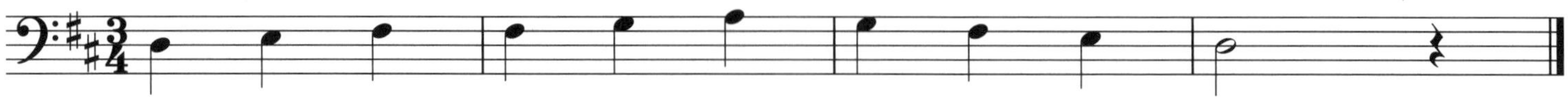

Grade 1 Stage 2

Set 2: Half position (B♭ major)

Prepared piece (first position)

1 What is the key? Play the scale and say the note names.
2 What will you count? Tap the rhythm of the piece.
3 What is similar about bars 2 and 3?
4 How does the final bar differ from the other bars?
5 How will you put some character into your performance?

Prepared piece (half position)

1 How many beats are in each bar?
2 Do any bars contain the same rhythm patterns?
3 Tap the rhythm then, tapping the pulse, hear the rhythm in your head.
4 What is similar about the melodic pattern in bars 1 and 3?
5 How will you put some character into your performance?

Improvise!

Make up your own piece (it can be as long or short as you like), beginning with one of these patterns. Make sure you keep the pulse steady.

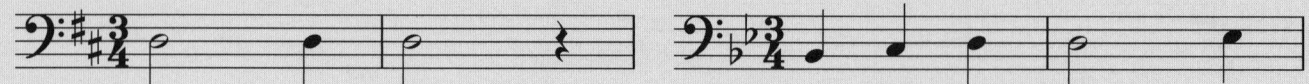

Now make up your own piece in D major or B♭ major, using any patterns you like.

Grade 1 **Stage 2**

Going solo!

Remember to prepare each piece carefully before you play it.

First position

Grade 1 **Stage 3**

Dynamic markings
♫ 2/4

Rhythmic exercises

Always remember to count two bars in.

1 2

3 4

5

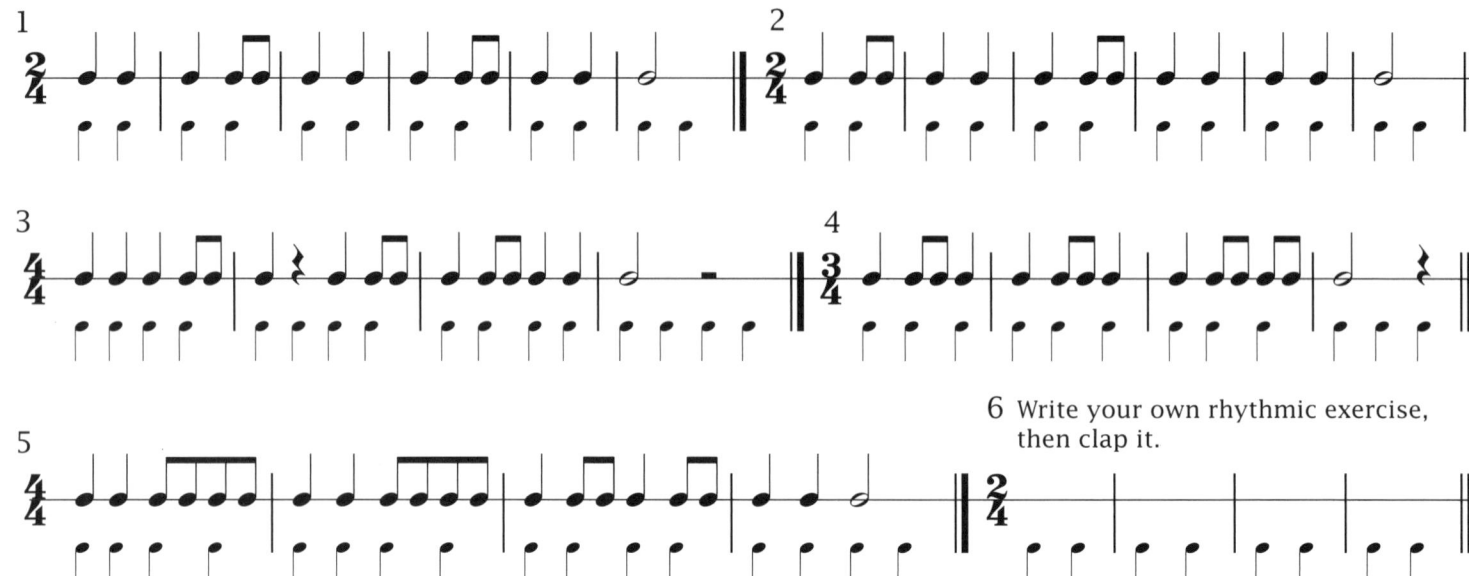

6 Write your own rhythmic exercise, then clap it.

Melodic exercises

Set 1: ♫ in first position

1

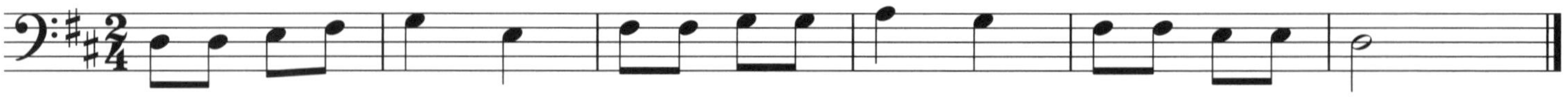

2

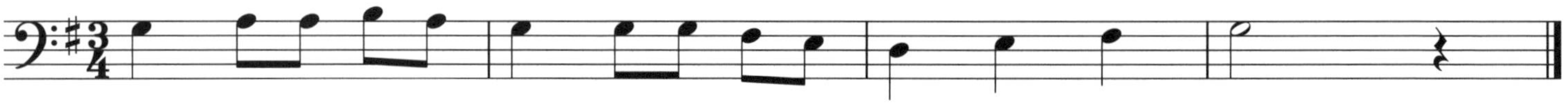

3

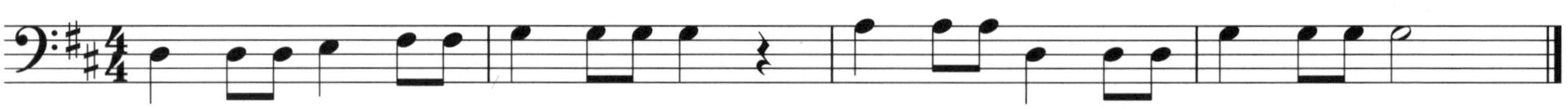

Set 2: ♫ in half position

4

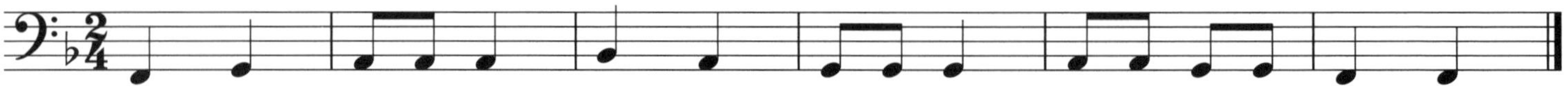

5

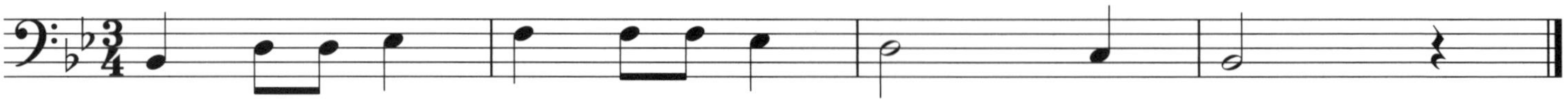

6

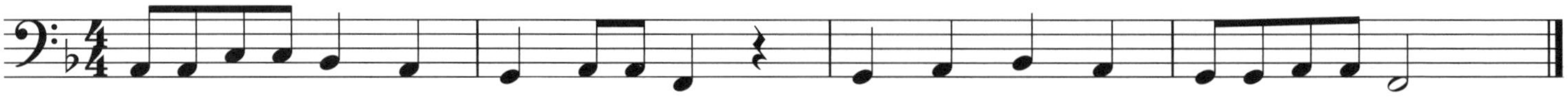

Grade 1 **Stage 3**

Prepared pieces (first position)

1 How many beats are there in each bar?
2 Do any bars contain the same rhythmic patterns?
3 Tap the rhythm then (tapping the pulse) hear the rhythm in your head.
4 How will you put some character into your performance?

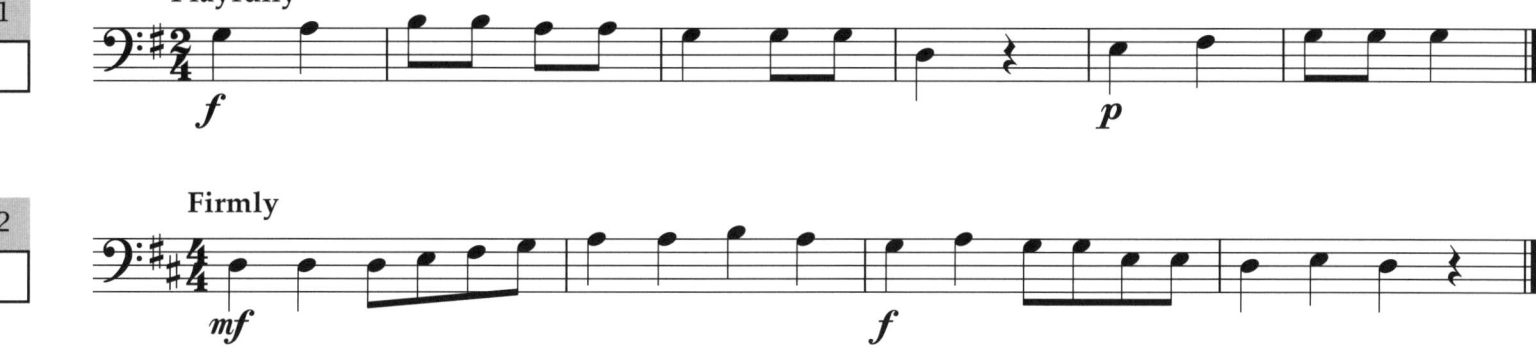

Prepared pieces (half position)

1 What is the key? Play the scale and say the note names.
2 What will you count? Tap the rhythm of the piece.
3 What do the two dynamic markings tell you?
4 Play the first note, then hear the piece in your head, with dynamics.

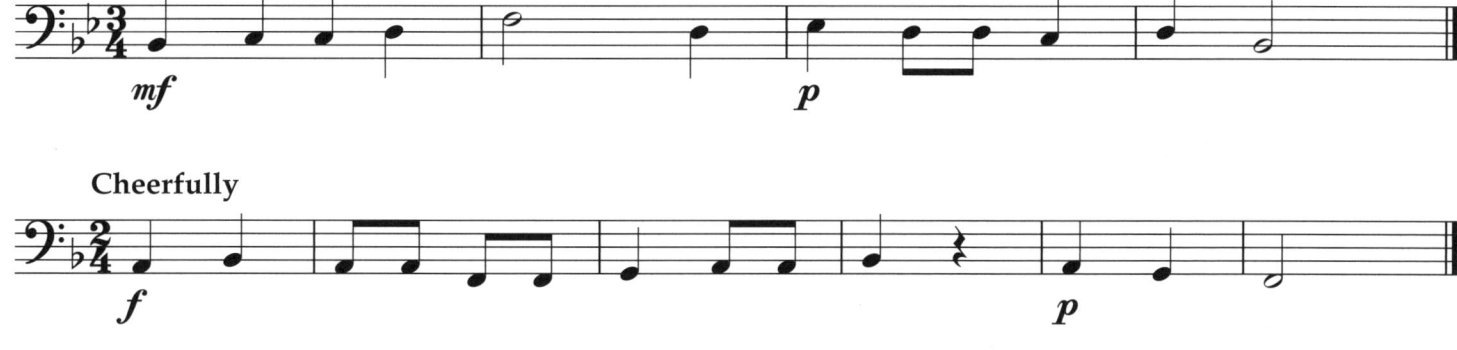

Improvise!

Make up your own piece (it can be as long or short as you like), beginning with one of these patterns. Make sure you keep the pulse steady.

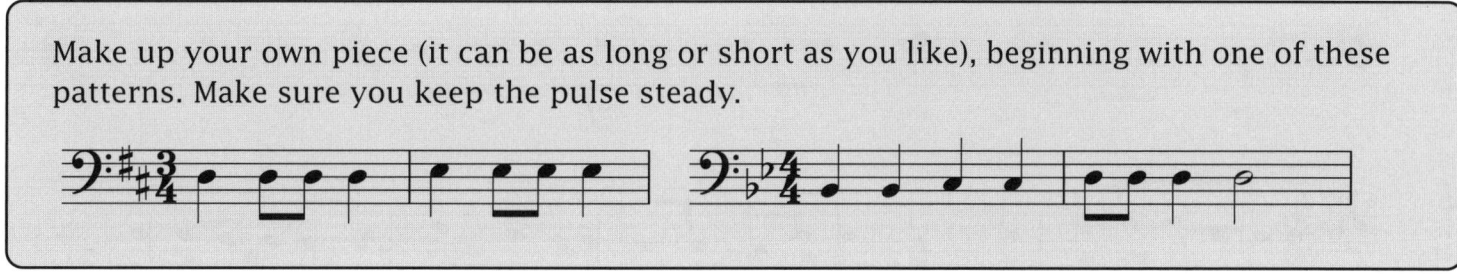

Grade 2 **Stage 1**

G and D major
2-note slurs

Rhythmic exercises

Always remember to count two bars in.

1

2

3

4

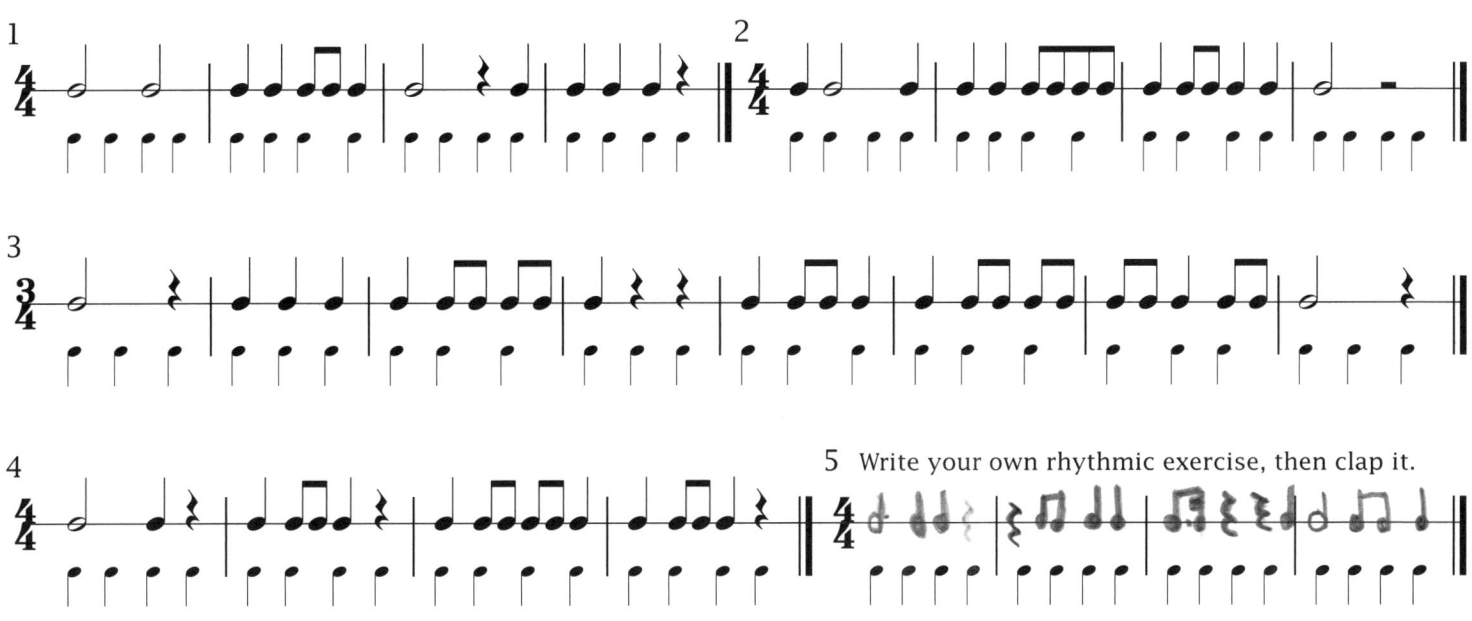

5 Write your own rhythmic exercise, then clap it.

Melodic exercises

1

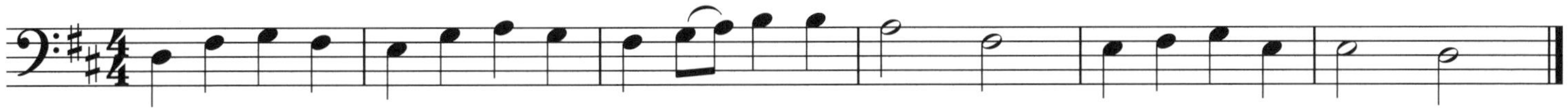

2

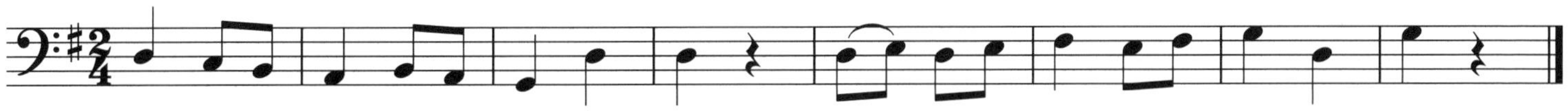

3

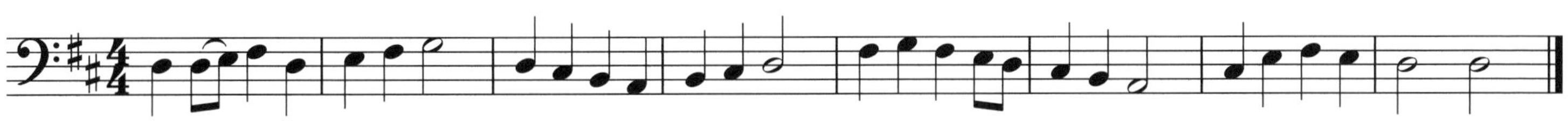

4

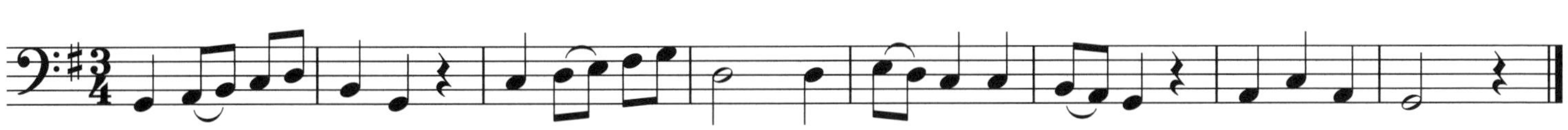

5

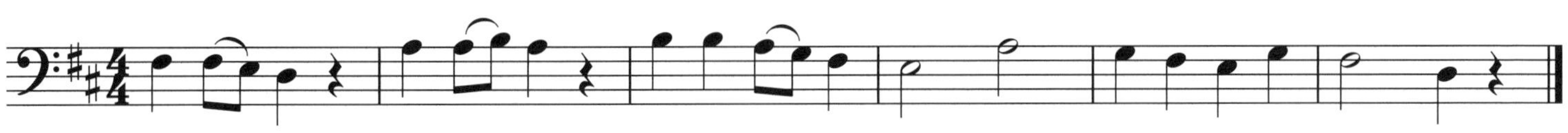

6

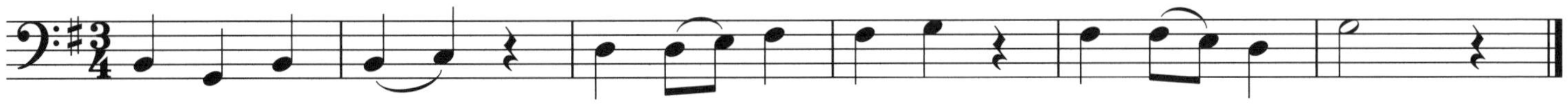

Prepared pieces

> 1 What will you count? Tap the pulse and hear the rhythm in your head.
> 2 What is the key? Play the scale and arpeggio in a dancing style.
> 3 What is the interval between the first two notes called? To which pattern do they belong?
> 4 Play the first note and try to hear the piece in your head.
> 5 How will you put character into your performance?

1

> 1 How will you count this piece? Hear the pulse in your head and tap the rhythm.
> 2 In which key is the piece? Play the scale and arpeggio with a gentle character.
> 3 The first two notes belong to the arpeggio – how many other patterns are there from the arpeggio?
> 4 How many bars share the same rhythm as bar 2?
> 5 How will you put expression into your performance?

2

Improvise!

1

> Make up your own piece (it can be as long or short as you like), beginning with this pattern. Decide on a mood or character before you begin.
>
>
>
> Now make up your own piece in D major – use any patterns you like.

2

Grade 2 Stage 1

Going solo! Remember to prepare each piece carefully before you play it.

Grade 2 Stage 2

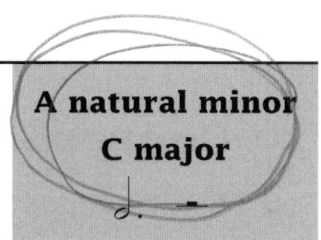

Rhythmic exercises

Always remember to count two bars in.

5 Write your own rhythmic exercise, then clap it.

Melodic exercises

Set 1: A minor

Set 2: C major

Grade 2 Stage 2

Prepared pieces

1. What is the key of this piece? Play the scale and arpeggio heavily.
2. What is the interval formed by the first two notes? Play the notes. Is there another example of this interval?
3. What is similar about bars 1 and 2? Are there any more similar bars?
4. Play the first note then study the first two bars for a few moments. Hear them in your head, then play them from memory.
5. How will you put character into your performance?

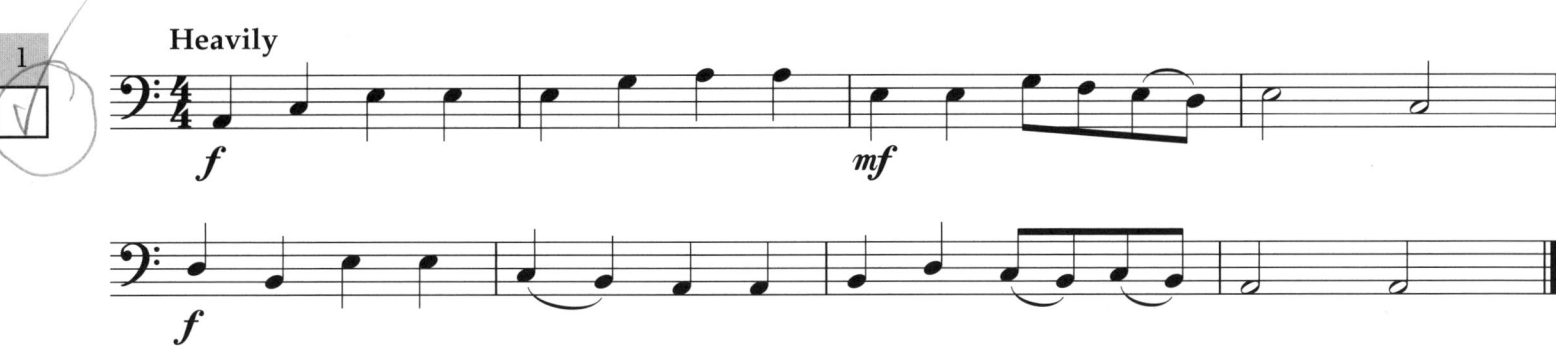

1. Play the scale and arpeggio elegantly.
2. Compare bars 2 and 6.
3. Count in your head and tap the rhythm.
4. Play the first note and try to hear the piece in your head.
5. How will you convey the character of this piece?

Improvise!

Make up your own piece (it can be as long or short as you like), beginning with this pattern. Decide on a mood or character before you begin.

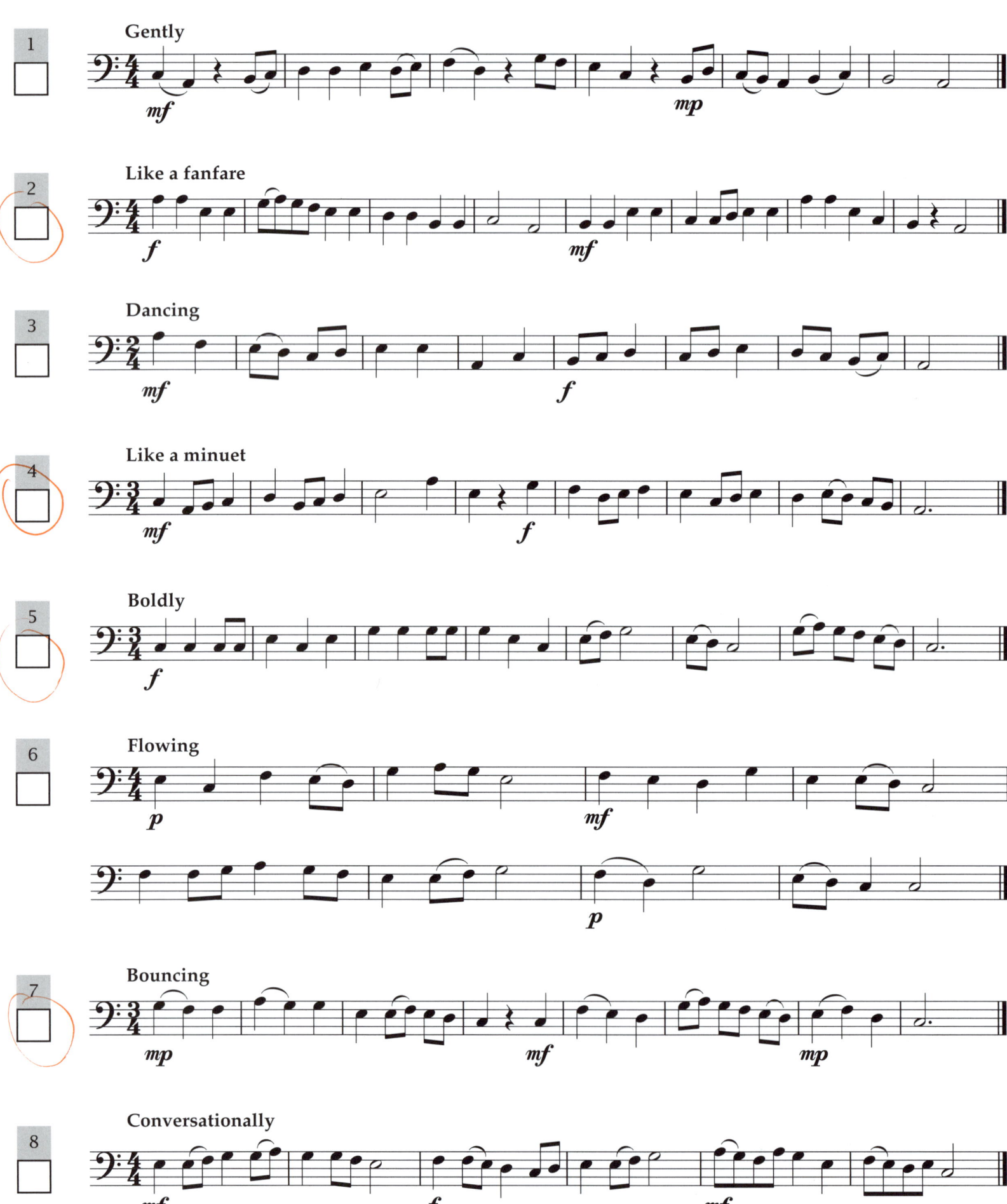

Grade 2 Stage 3

Revision

Rhythmic exercises

Always remember to count two bars in.

5 Write your own rhythmic exercise, then clap it.

Melodic exercises

Prepared pieces

> 1. What is the key of this piece? Play the scale and arpeggio in a grand, fanfare style.
> 2. How many times does the rhythmic pattern in bar 1 return?
> 3. To what pattern do the notes in bars 1 and 2 belong?
> 4. Read the piece through, hearing it in your head.
> 5. What is the character of the music? How will you put that character into your performance?

1

> 1. Think through the bowing in your head.
> 2. Have a quick look through the piece. Do you feel you understand it?
> 3. Count in your head and tap the rhythm.
> 4. Play the first note and hear the piece through in your head.
> 5. What are the clues to the character of this piece?

2

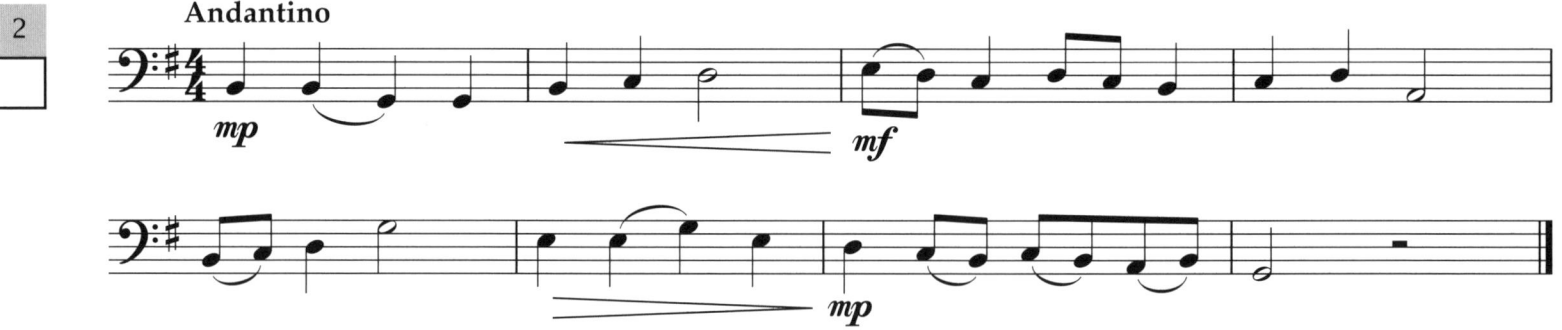

Improvise!

> Make up your own piece (it can be as long or short as you like), beginning with this pattern. Decide on a mood or character before you begin.
>
>

Grade 3 Stage 1

F major (half position)

Ties ♩. ♪

Rhythmic exercises

Each set of exercises go **downwards**. In set 2, *feel* the tied notes strongly, but don't play them. In the dotted rhythm in set 3 you should still feel the 'tied' note, even though it has become a dot!

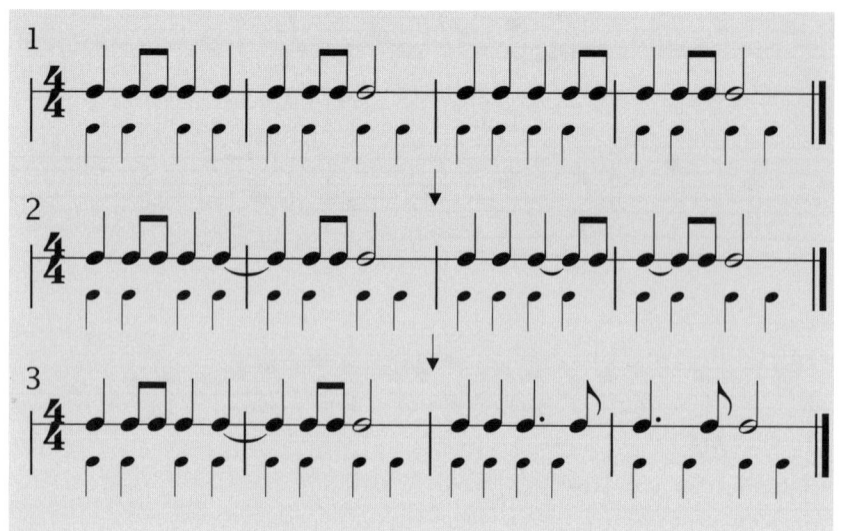
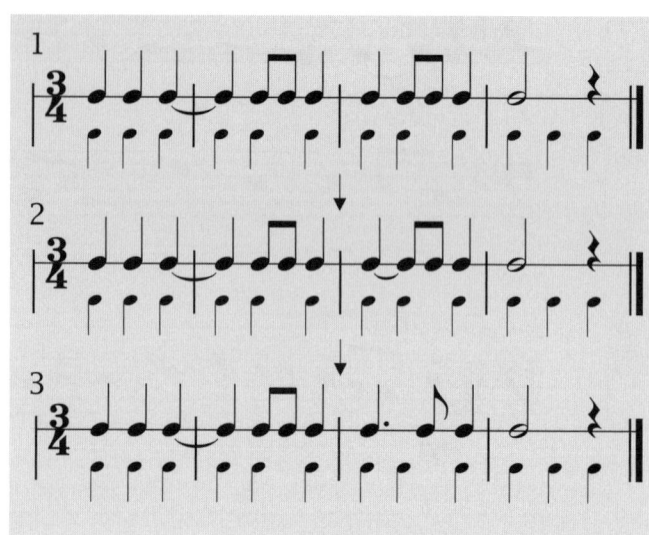

Melodic exercises

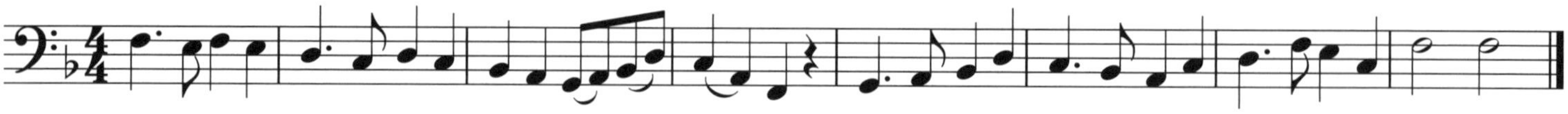

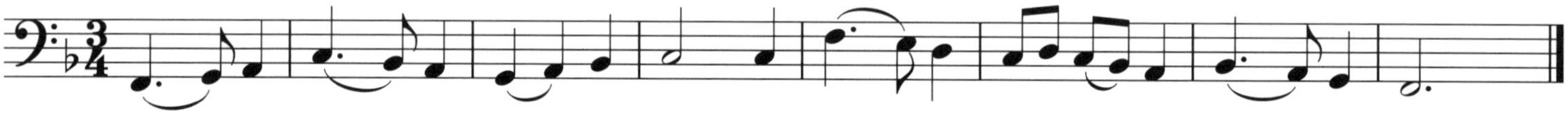

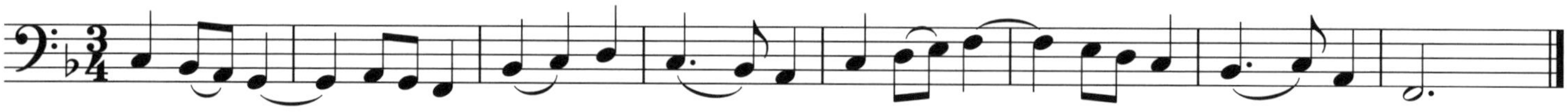

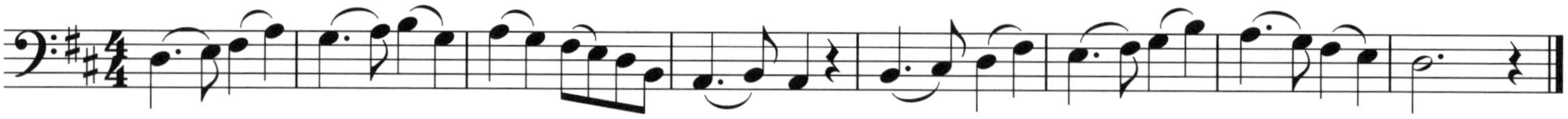

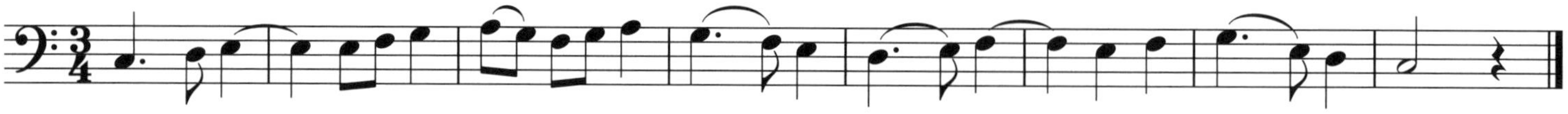

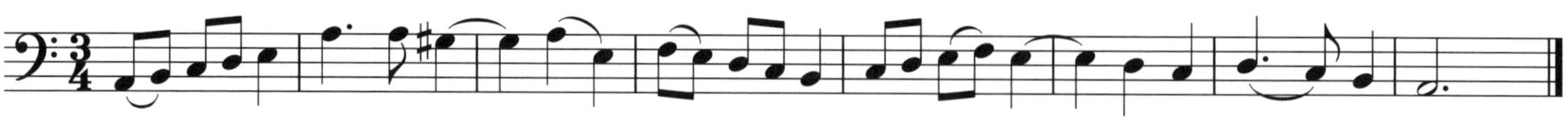

Grade 3 **Stage 1**

Prepared pieces

> 1 What is the key of this piece? Play the scale and arpeggio gracefully.
> 2 How many scale or arpeggio patterns can you find?
> 3 Does the rhythm in bar 1 appear again? Hear bars 1–2 in your head while tapping the pulse.
> 4 Tap the pulse and think the rhythm of the piece, then tap the rhythm and think the pulse.
> 5 Play the first note and hear the piece in your head, including musical expression.

1

> 1 In which key is this piece? Play the scale and arpeggio expressively. On which degree of the scale does the piece begin?
> 2 What connects the first notes of bars 1, 2, 3 and 4?
> 3 Think through the bowing.
> 4 Tap the pulse with one hand and the rhythm with the other. Repeat, swapping hands.
> 5 How will you put character into your performance?

2

Improvise!

> Now make up your own piece (it can be as long or short as you like), beginning with this pattern. Decide on a mood or character before you begin.
>
>

Going solo! Remember to prepare each piece carefully before you play it.

Grade 3 Stage 2

B♭ major

Rhythmic exercises

Always remember to count two bars in.

Melodic exercises

Prepared pieces

> 1 Look through this piece. Do you feel you understand it?
> 2 Look carefully at the patterns. How much is based on scale and arpeggio patterns?
> 3 Play the scale *f* and arpeggio *mp*.
> 4 Think through the bowing carefully.
> 5 Play the first note and hear the piece in your head, including musical expression.

1

> 1 In which key is this piece? Play the scale and arpeggio *mf* then *p*.
> 2 How many repeating patterns can you find?
> 3 What is special about bars 5–6?
> 4 Tap the pulse with your hands and the rhythm with your foot. Then swap.
> 5 How will you put character into your performance?

2

Improvise!

> Now make up your own piece (it can be as long or short as you like), beginning with this pattern. Decide on a mood or character before you begin.
>
>

Grade 3 **Stage 2**

Going solo! Remember to prepare each piece carefully before you play it.

Grade 3 **Stage 3**

B minor
Staccato and pizzicato

Rhythmic exercises

Always remember to count two bars in.

1

2

3

Melodic exercises

1

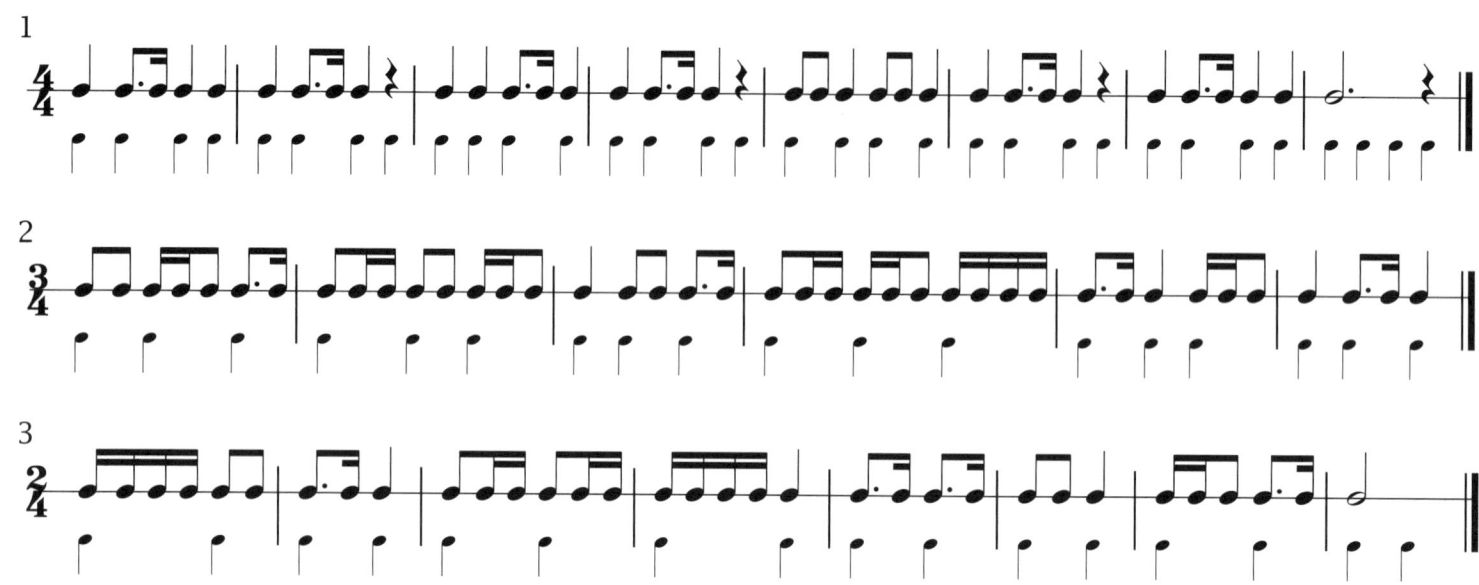

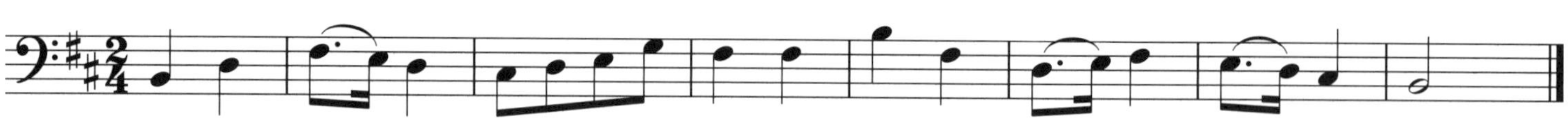

2

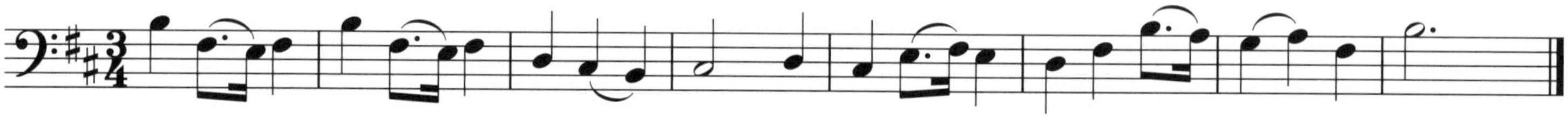

3

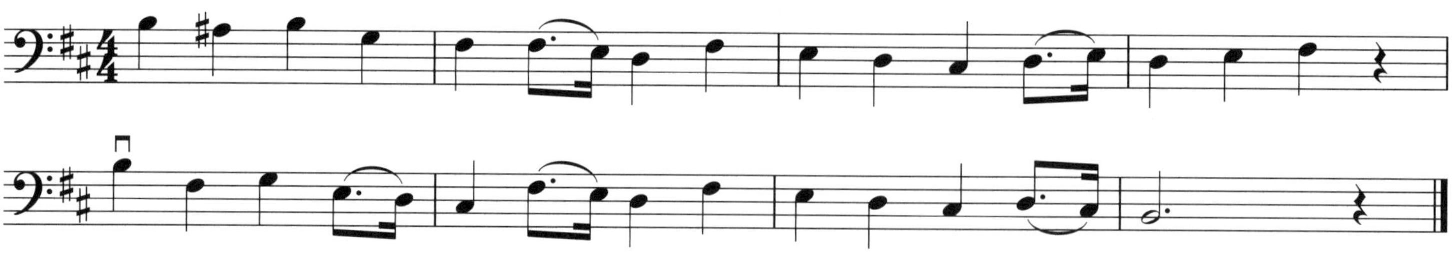

4

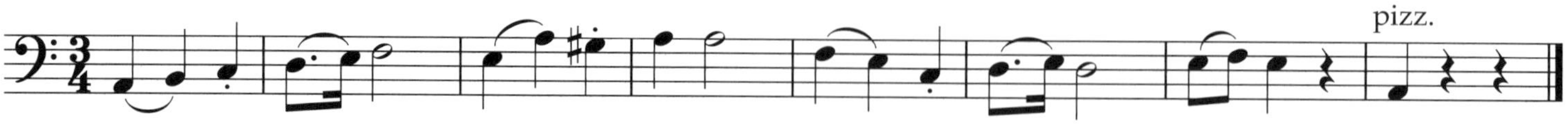

5

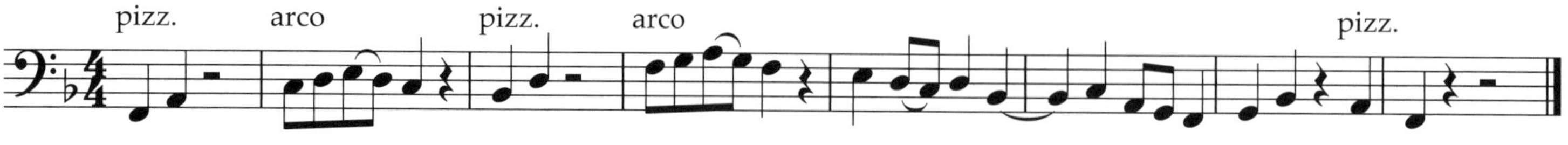

Grade 3 **Stage 3**

Prepared pieces

> 1 In which key is this piece? Play the scale and arpeggio elegantly.
> 2 Think carefully about the rhythm. Are you certain you know how it goes?
> 3 Play the rhythm of the piece on one note of your choice.
> 4 Think through the bowing.
> 5 Play the first note then hear the piece in your head, including musical expression.

1

> 1 In which key is this piece? Play the scale and arpeggio.
> 2 How much of this piece is based on scale patterns?
> 3 Think through the fingering.
> 4 Tap the pulse with one hand and the rhythm with the other. Repeat, swapping hands.
> 5 How will you put character into your performance?

2

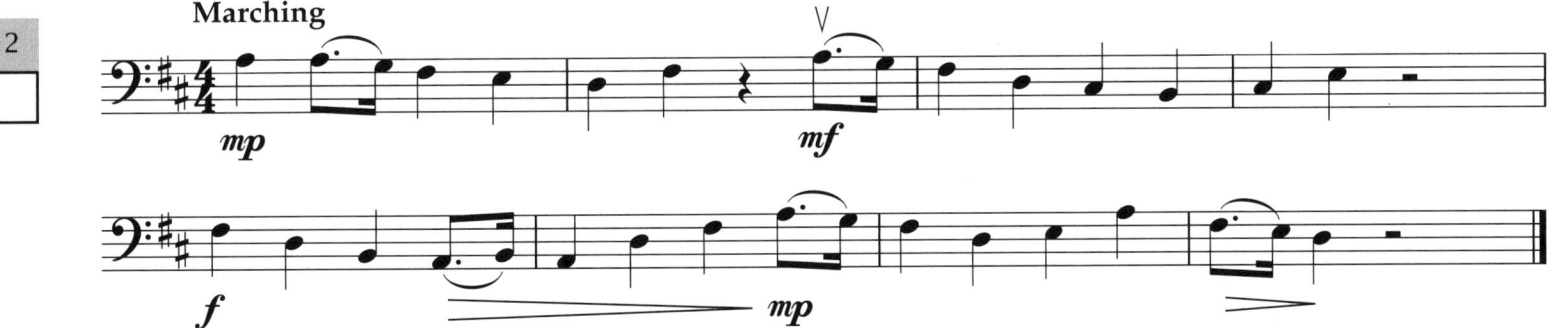

Improvise!

> Make up your own piece (it can be as long or short as you like), beginning with this pattern. Decide on a mood or character before you begin.
>
>

Going solo! Remember to prepare each piece carefully before you play it.

Grade 4 **Stage 1**

A major
Shifting to 3rd position
Upbeats

Rhythmic exercises

Always remember to count two bars in.

1

2

3

Melodic exercises

1

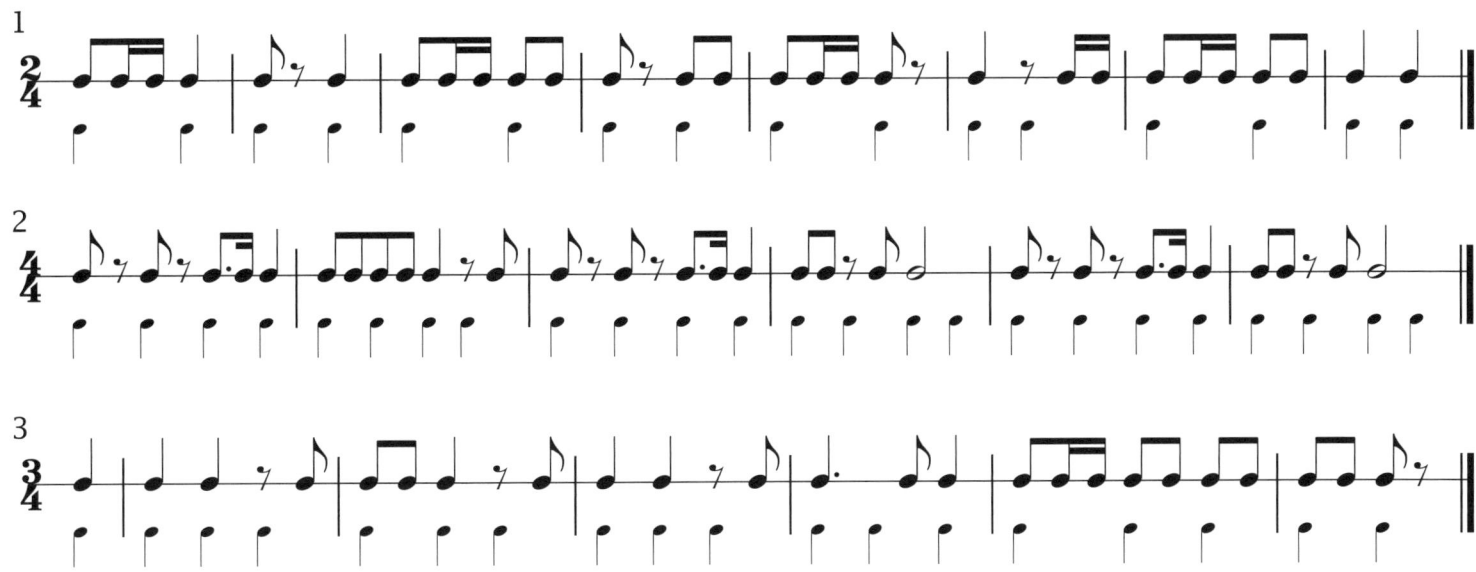

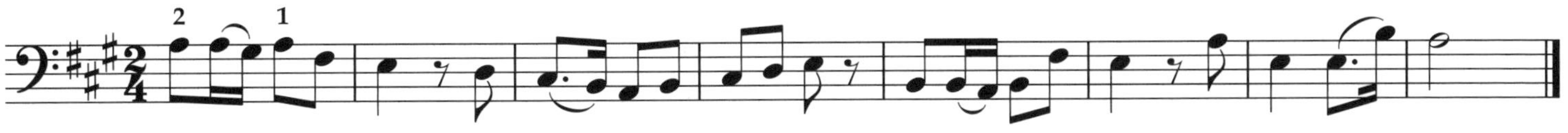

2

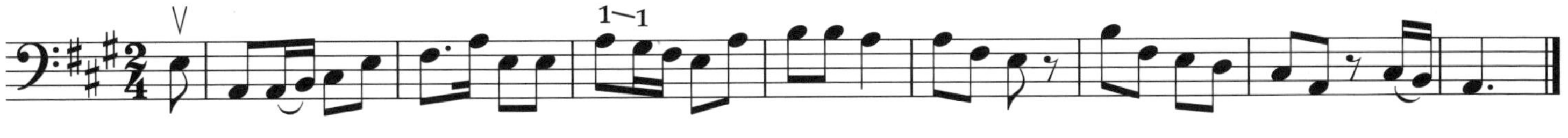

3

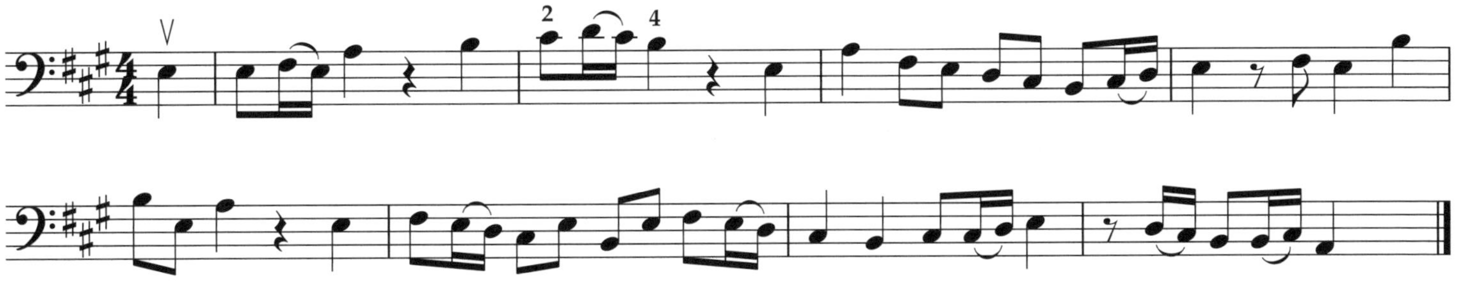

4

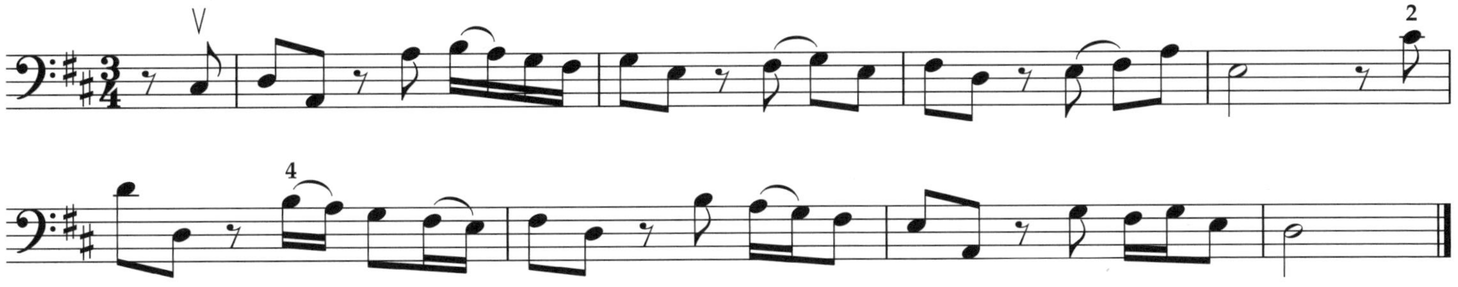

Prepared pieces

> 1 Play the scale of this key *mf* ascending and *p* descending, and then the arpeggio *f*.
> 2 Look for groups of notes that belong to the scale and arpeggio.
> 3 Have you spotted where you will need to shift?
> 4 What will you count? Tap the pulse strongly and think the rhythm, then tap the rhythm softly and think the pulse.
> 5 Play the first note then hear the piece in your head, including musical expression.

1

> 1 In which key is this piece? Play the scale and arpeggio.
> 2 Fill in the missing word: this piece begins with an _____
> 3 Set a pulse going in your head and hear the piece through at the same time.
> 4 Check the fingering in bar 3: do you understand it?
> 5 How will you make your performance sound funny?

2

Improvise!

> Make up your own piece (it can be as long or short as you like), beginning with this pattern. Decide on a mood or character before you begin.
>
>

Grade 4 **Stage 1**

Going solo! Remember to prepare each piece carefully before you play it.

Grade 4 Stage 2

$\frac{6}{8}$ rhythm patterns
D minor

Rhythmic exercises

Always remember to count two bars in.

1

2

3

Melodic exercises

1

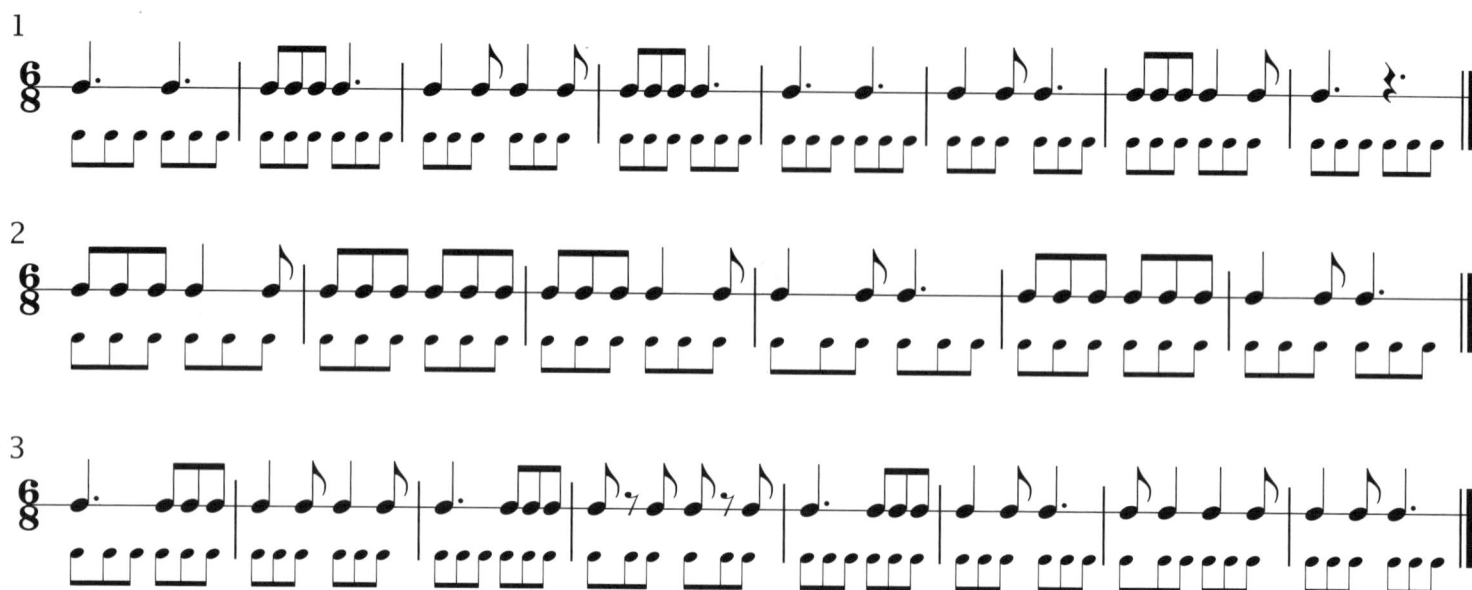

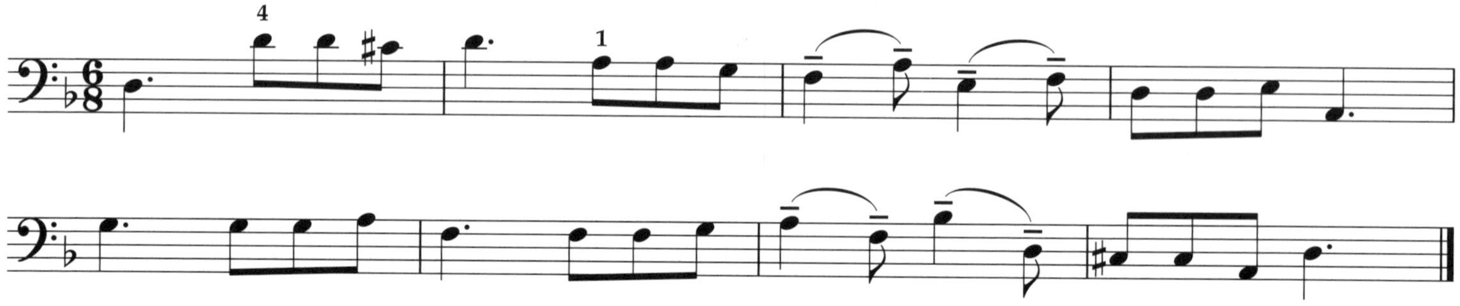

2

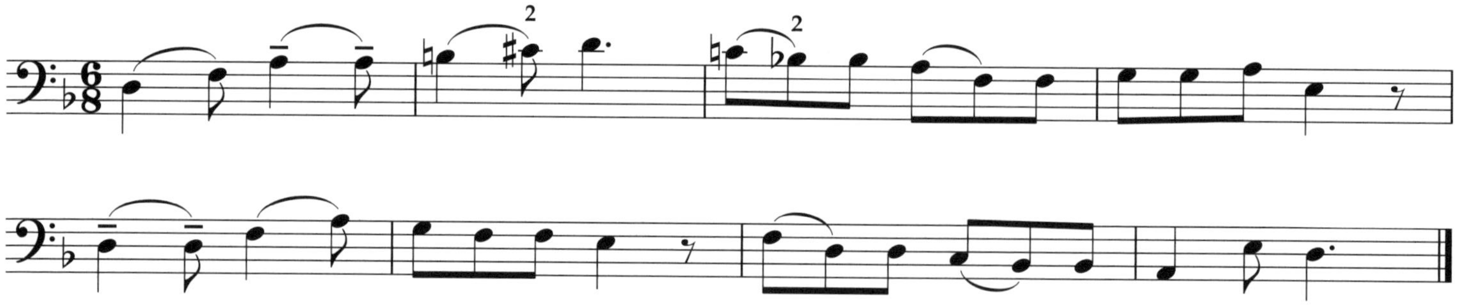

3

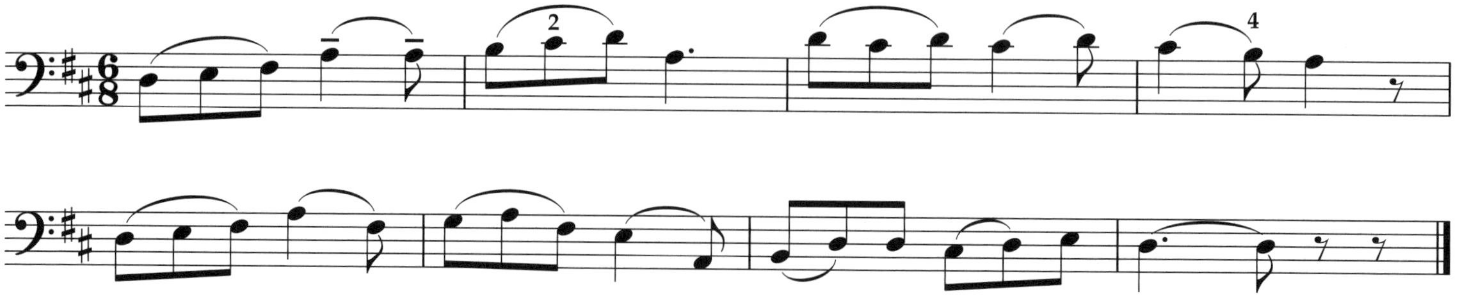

Grade 4 **Stage 2**   35

Prepared pieces

> 1 Play the scale slowly and gracefully.
> 2 Do any bars have the same rhythm?
> 3 Set the pulse going in your head then tap the rhythm.
> 4 Study any two bars for a few moments, then play them from memory. Try using them as a starting point for an improvisation.
> 5 Play the first note then hear the piece in your head.

1

> 1 In which key is this piece? Play the scale slowly and heavily.
> 2 Do any bars have the same rhythm?
> 3 Choose two bars and then use them as the start of an improvisation. Make use of ingredients from the piece in your improvisation.
> 4 Study any two-bar phrase for a few moments and then play it from memory.
> 5 Play the first note and then hear the piece in your head.

2

Going solo! Remember to prepare each piece carefully before you play it.

Grade 4 **Stage 3**

More 6/8 rhythm patterns
E minor

Rhythmic exercises

Always remember to count two bars in.

1

2

3

Melodic exercises

1
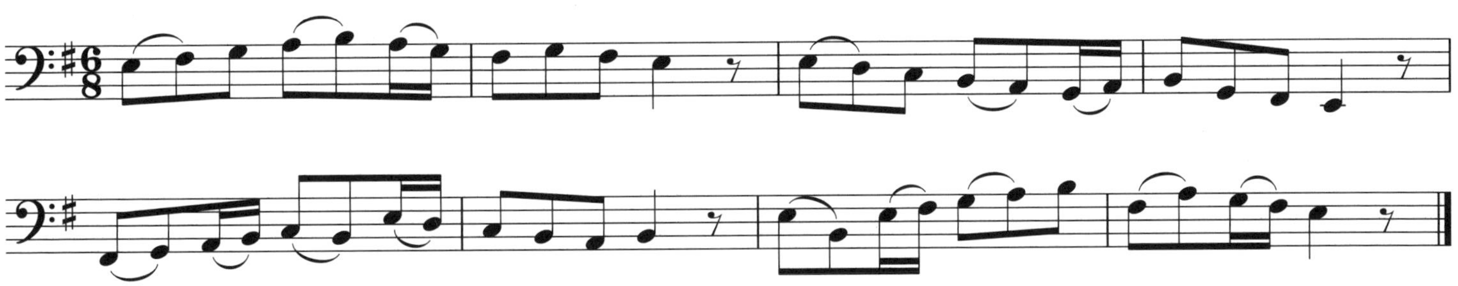

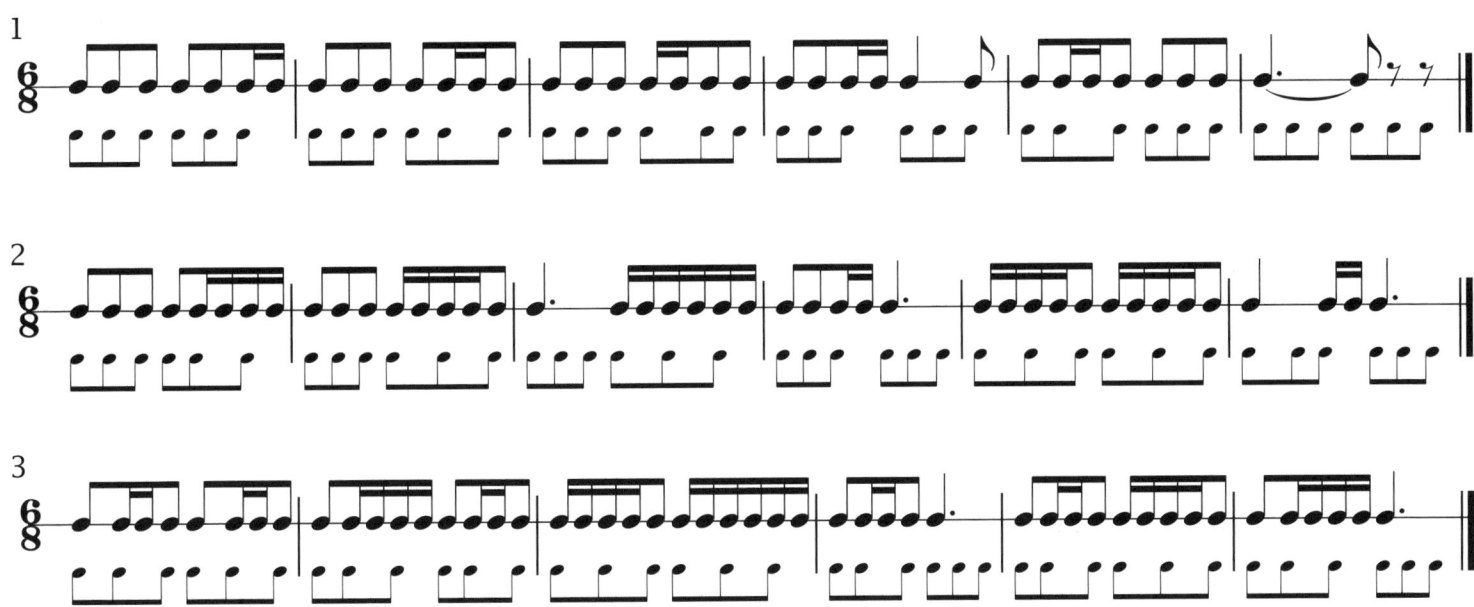

2
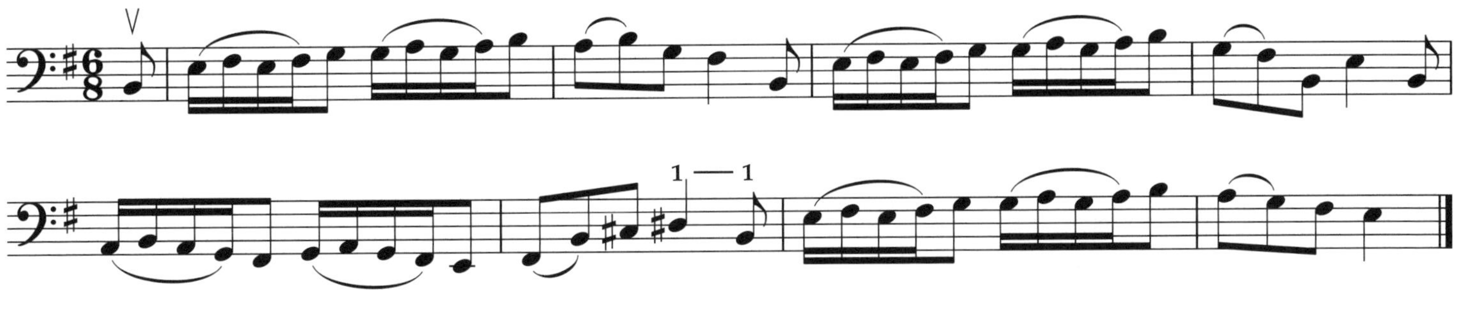

3
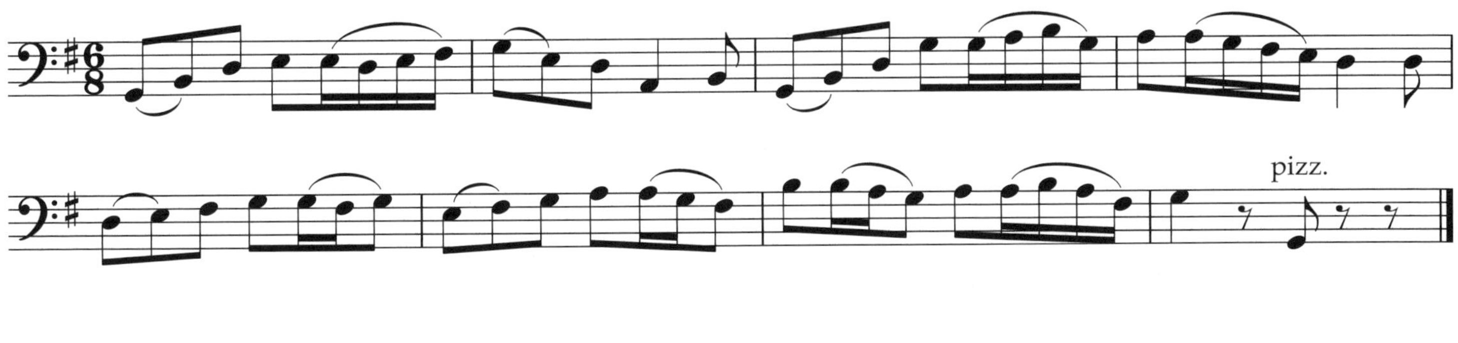

Prepared pieces

> 1 Play the scale of the piece *mf* ascending and *f* descending.
> 2 What is a reel? Using some of the rhythms from the piece improvise your own reel.
> 3 Think through the bowing and bow speed.
> 4 What will you count? Tap the pulse strongly and think the rhythm, then tap the rhythm softly and think the pulse.
> 5 Play the first note then hear the piece in your head, including musical expression.

> 1 In which key is this piece? Play the scale slowly, with excellent intonation.
> 2 How many bars have the same rhythm?
> 3 Think the pulse in your head and tap the rhythm.
> 4 What do you notice about bars 5 and 6? Play these bars then see if you can continue the pattern.
> 5 Play the first note and then hear the piece in your head.

Grade 4 Stage 3

Going solo! Remember to prepare each piece carefully before you play it.

Grade 5 **Stage 1**

Dotted rhythms in $\frac{6}{8}$
More shifting

Rhythmic exercises

Always remember to count two bars in.

1

2

3

Melodic exercises

1

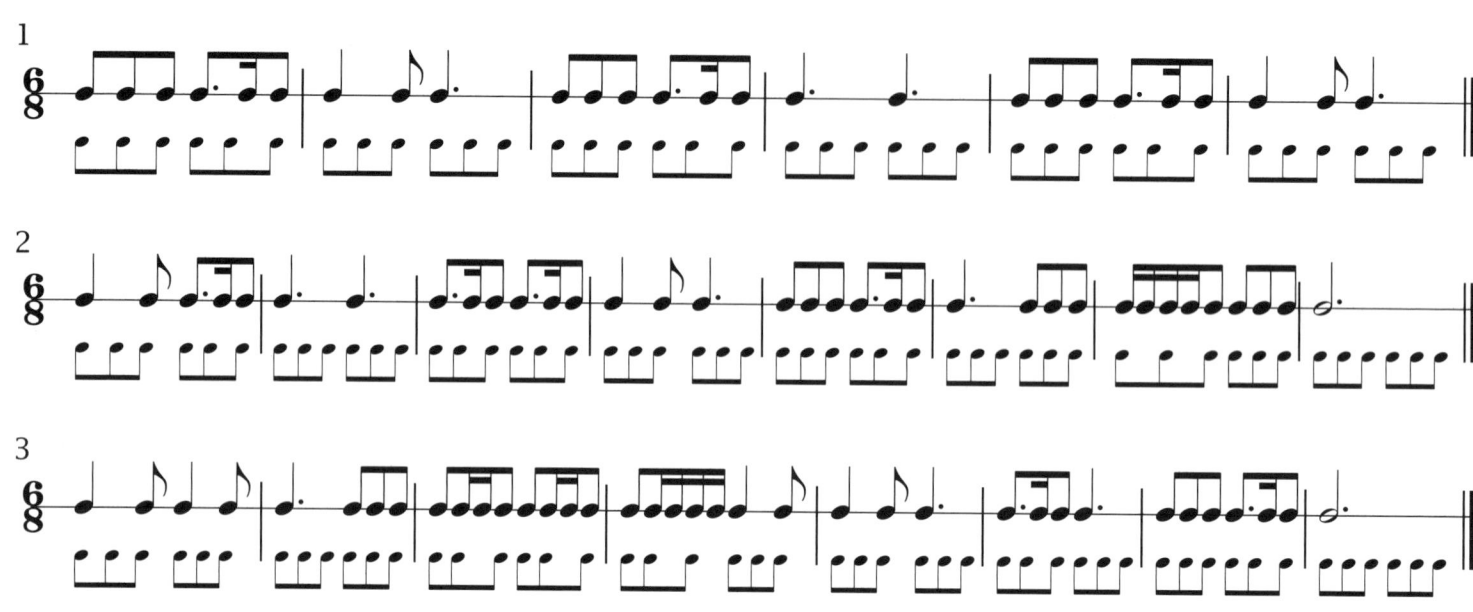

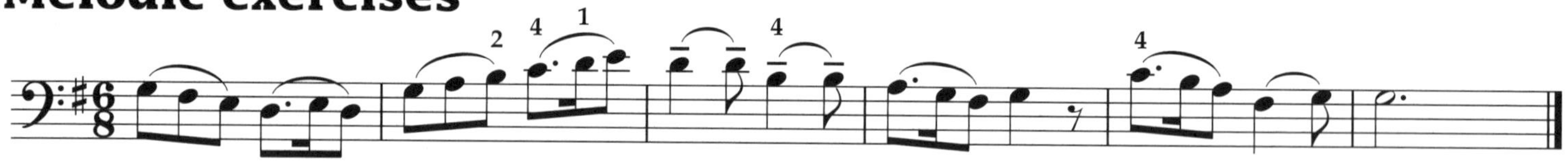

2

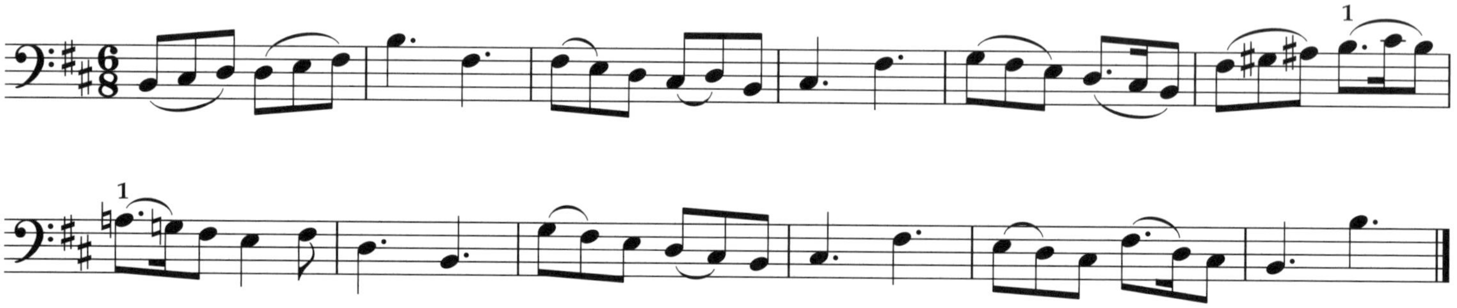

3

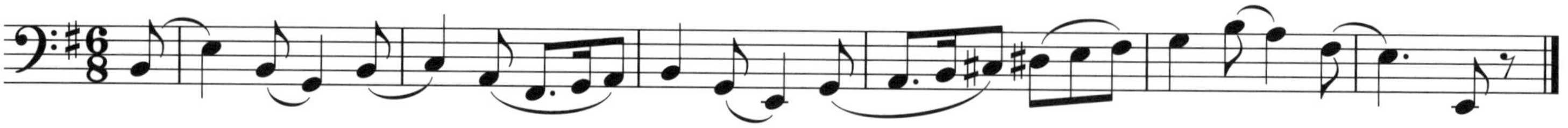

4

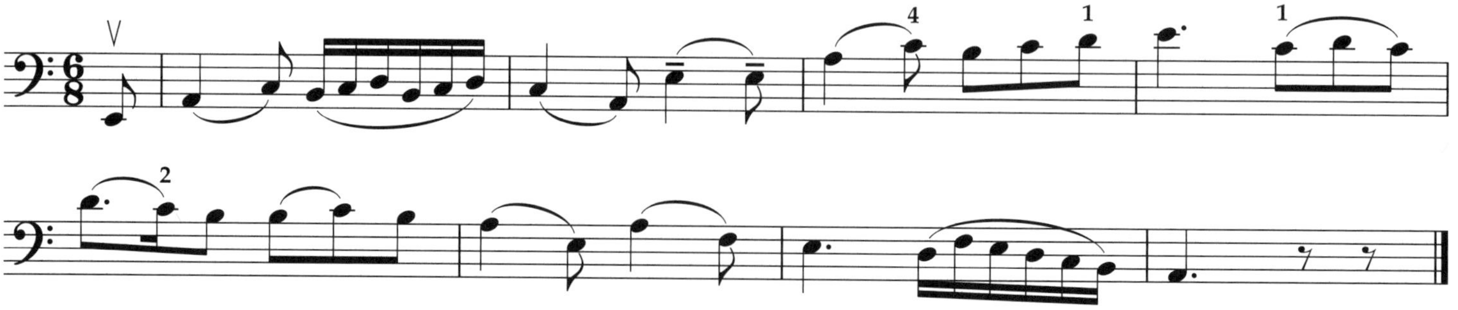

Prepared pieces

> 1. What is the key? Play the scale and arpeggio calmly, using dynamics from the piece.
> 2. Can you spot any repeated whole-bar rhythm patterns? Choose one and improvise a short piece based on it.
> 3. Think through the fingering of the whole piece.
> 4. What will you count? Tap the pulse strongly and think the rhythm, then tap the rhythm softly and think the pulse.
> 5. Play the first note then hear the piece in your head. When you feel you really know it, play it with confidence.

> 1. In which key is this piece? Play the scale and arpeggio with energy.
> 2. Walk around the room to the pulse, and sing the rhythm with gusto!
> 3. Think through the fingering. Where will you shift?
> 4. Choose a bar and make up an improvisation based on it.
> 5. Read through the piece as if it were a paragraph of text. When you understand how it goes, play it with confidence!

Grade 5 Stage 1

Going solo! Remember to prepare each piece carefully before you play it.

Grade 5 Stage 2

G minor

Rhythmic exercises

Always remember to count two bars in.

Melodic exercises

Prepared pieces

> 1 Play the scale and arpeggio softly, with a 'mesto' character.
> 2 To which pattern do the first three notes belong?
> 3 Choose an interesting rhythm from the piece and use it to improvise.
> 4 Tap the pulse strongly and think the rhythm, then tap the rhythm softly and think the pulse.
> 5 Play the first note then imagine playing the piece through confidently.

> 1 Play the scale with a *crescendo* ascending and a *diminuendo* descending.
> 2 How many repeated ideas can you find?
> 3 Choose an interesting rhythm from the piece and use it to improvise.
> 4 Study the first four bars for a few moments then play them from memory.
> 5 Play the first note then imagine playing the piece through confidently.

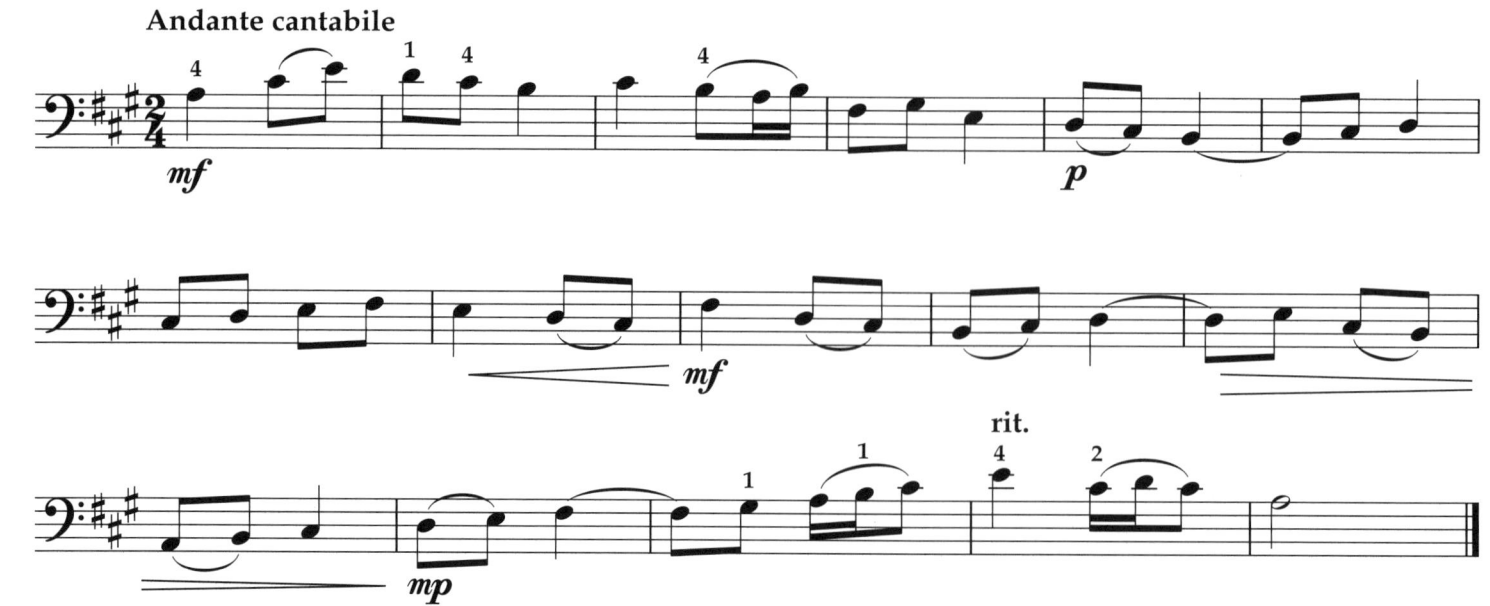

Grade 5 **Stage 2**

Going solo! Remember to prepare each piece carefully before you play it.

Grade 5 Stage 3

Simple syncopation

Rhythmic exercises

Always remember to count two bars in.

Melodic exercises

What do you notice about the following two exercises?

Grade 5 Stage 3

Prepared pieces

> 1 Play the scale with a *crescendo* ascending, a *diminuendo* descending and a *rit* at the end.
> 2 Think through the bowing, and in particular the bow speed.
> 3 What will you count? Tap the pulse strongly and think the rhythm, then tap the rhythm softly and think the pulse.
> 4 What is the character? How will you convey this?
> 5 Play the first note then hear the piece through in your head, complete with musical expression.

1

> 1 In which key is this piece? Play the scale cheerfully.
> 2 How many repeated ideas can you find?
> 3 Set a pulse going in your head and hear the piece through at the same time.
> 4 Study the first two bars for a few moments then play them from memory.
> 5 Do you feel you know how the piece goes? When you do, count a bar in and play it with real confidence.

2

Going solo! Remember to prepare each piece carefully before you play it.

With many thanks to Andrei Mihailescu and David Heyes for their invaluable help.

© 2013 by Faber Music Ltd
Bloomsbury House 74–77 Great Russell Street London WC1B 3DA
Music processed by MacMusic
Cover and page design by Susan Clarke
Cover illustration by Drew Hillier
Printed in England by Caligraving Ltd
All rights reserved

ISBN10: 0-571-53700-6
EAN13: 978-0-571-53700-6